Trains
and
Dinosaurs
COLORING BOOK

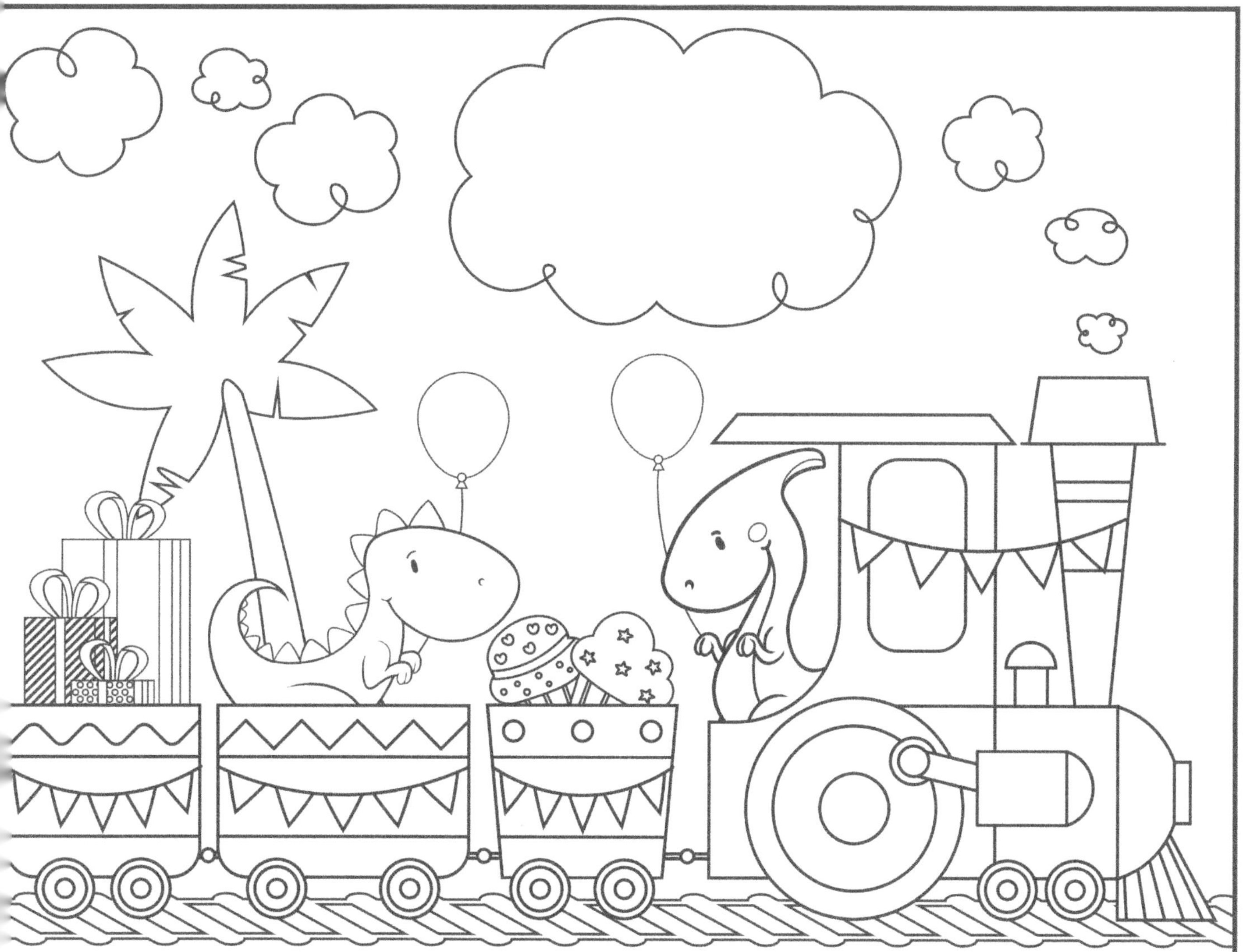

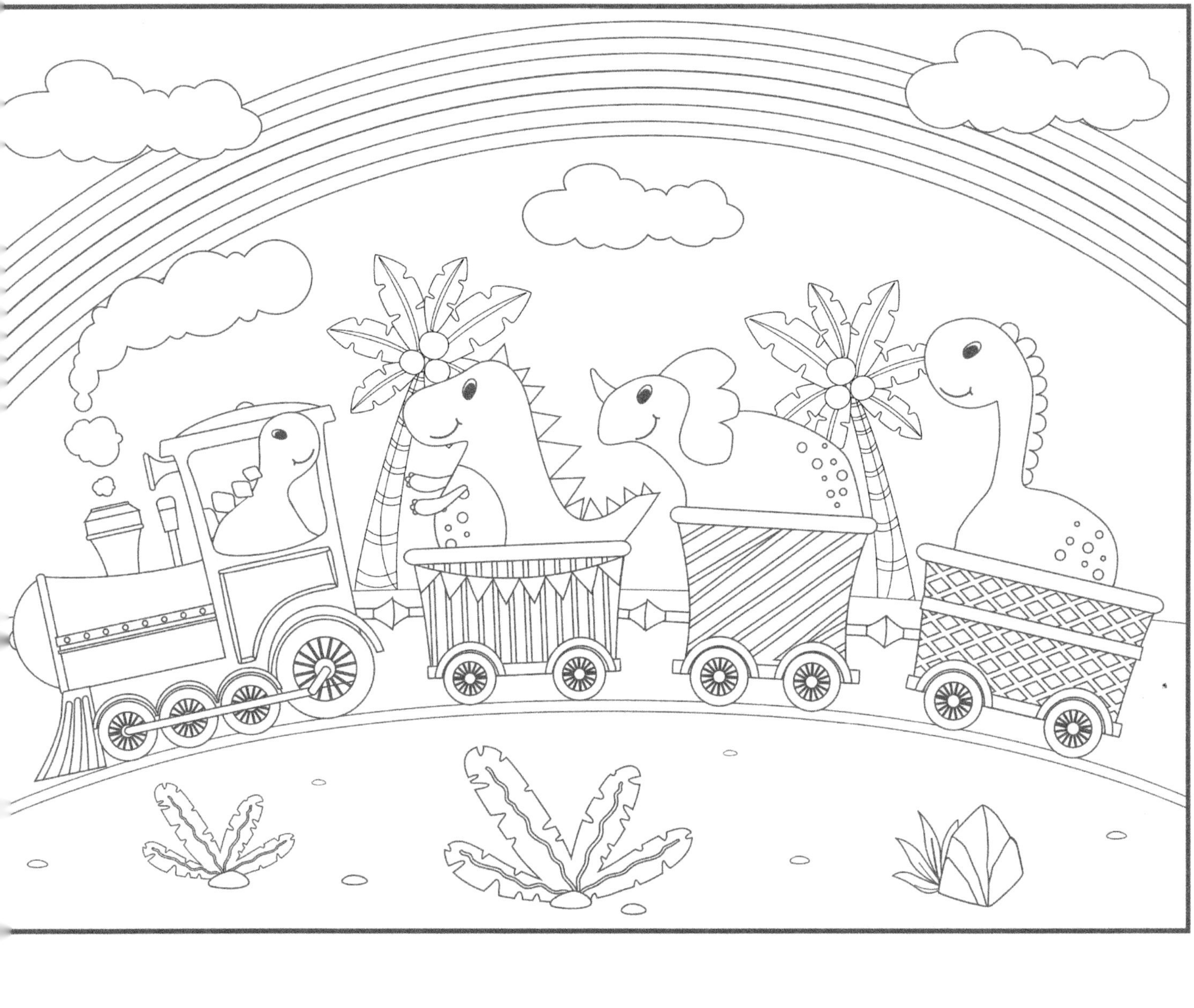

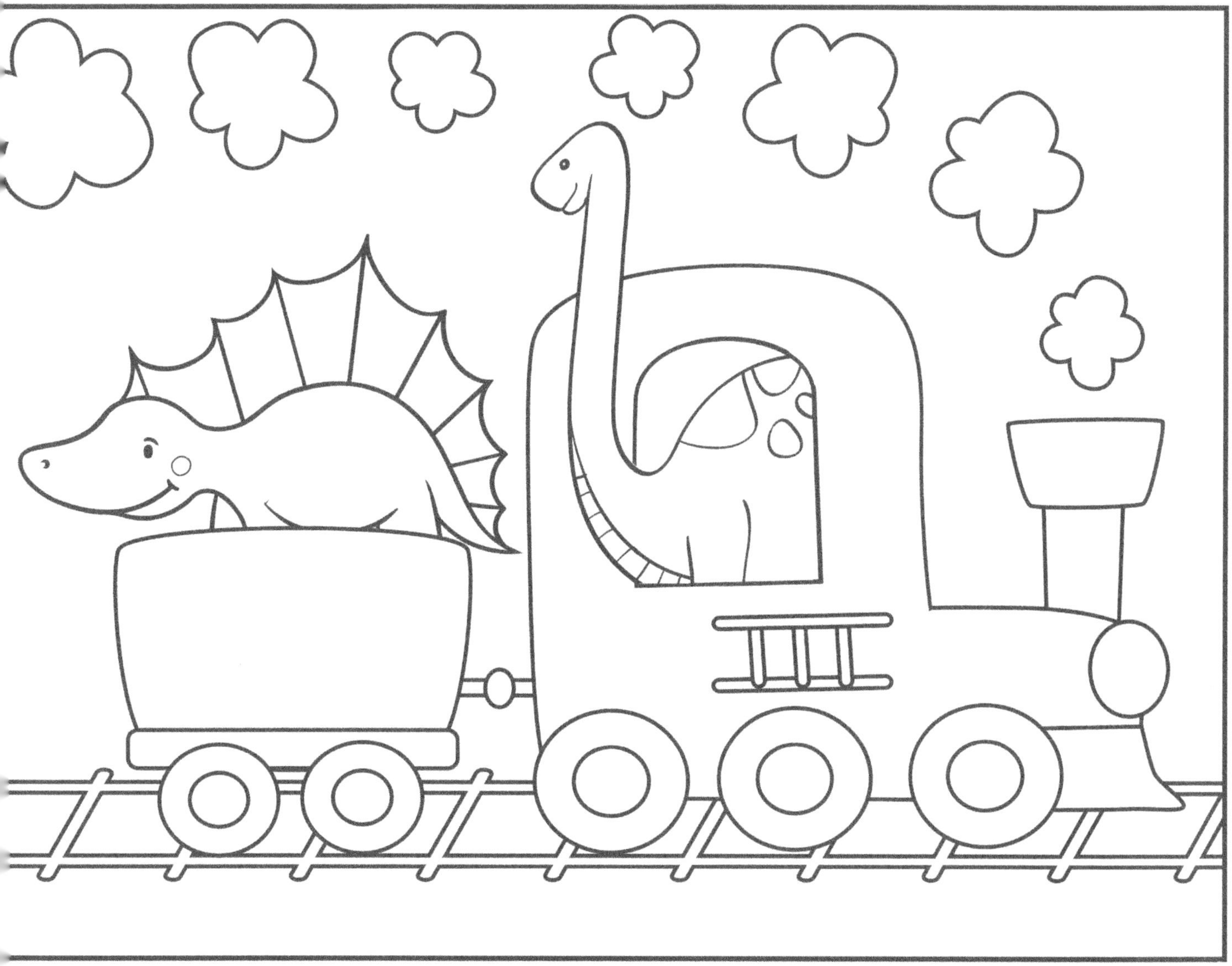

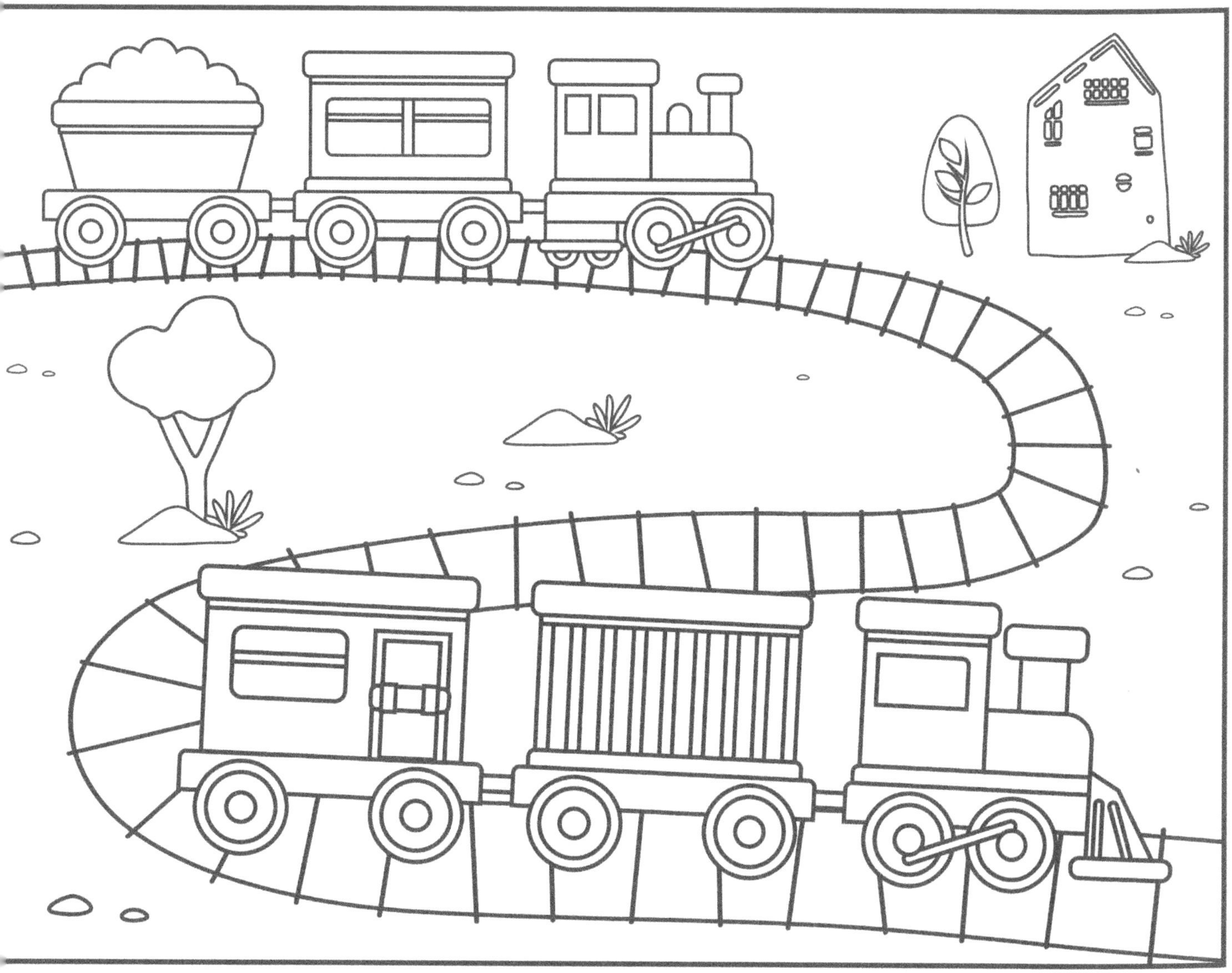

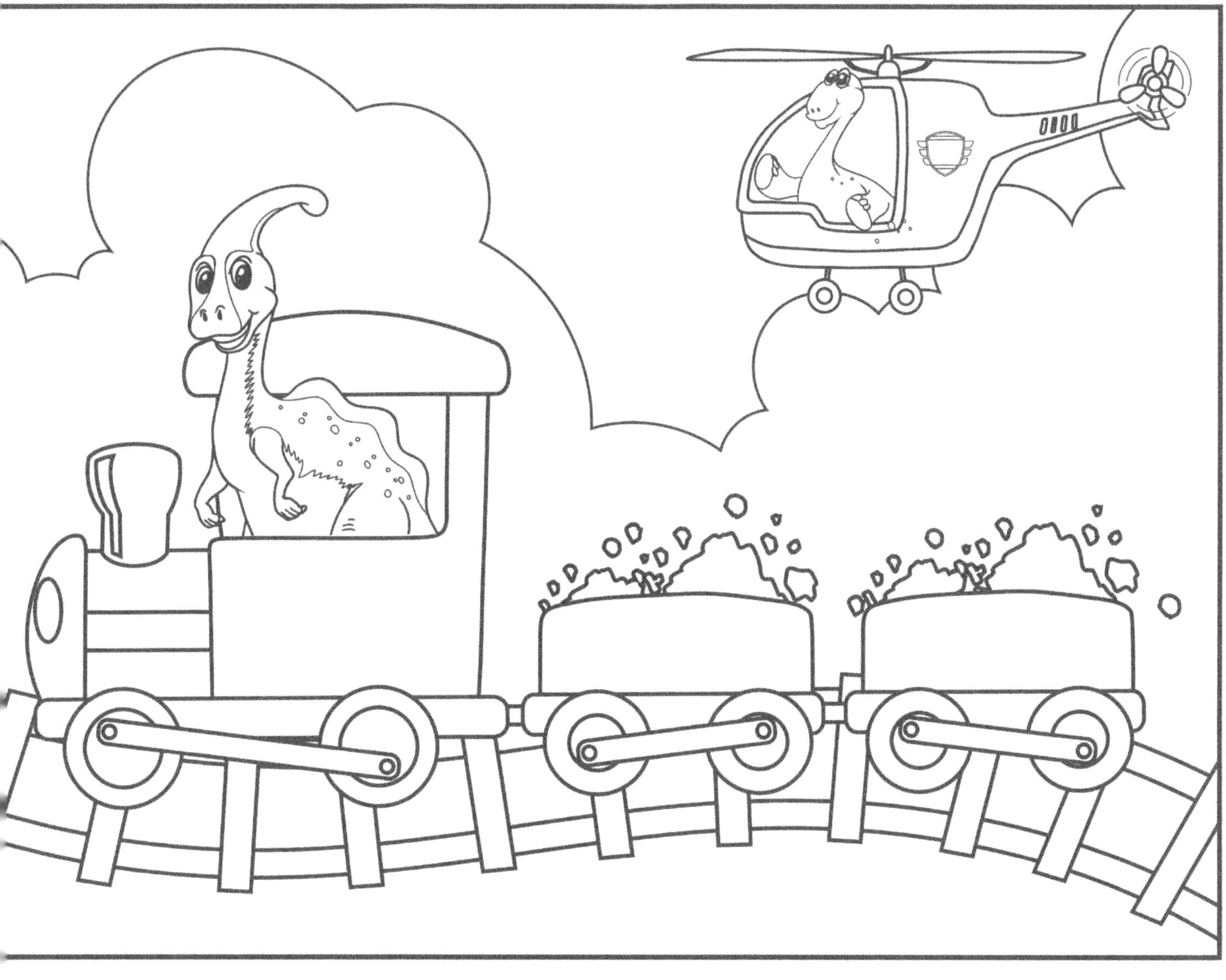

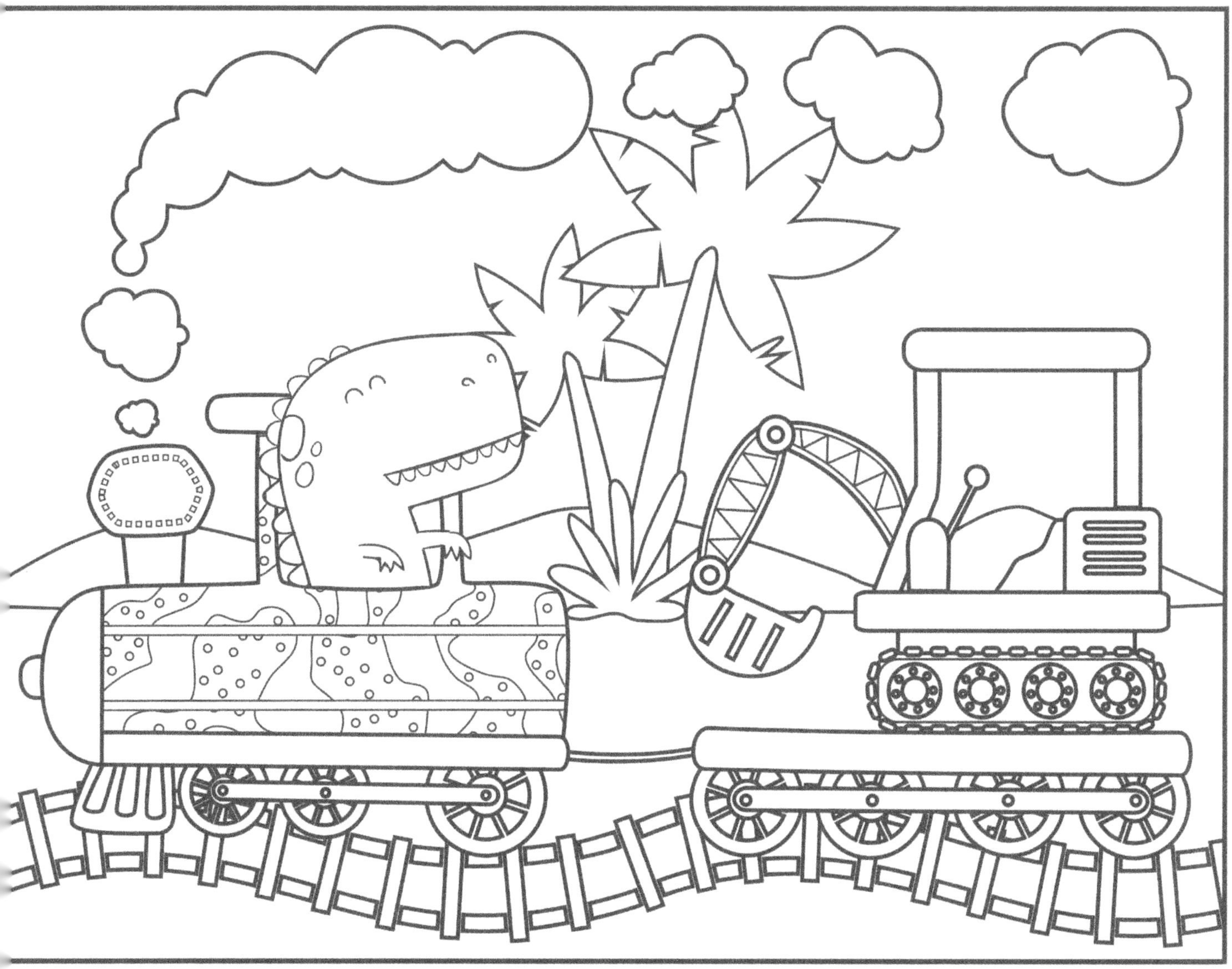

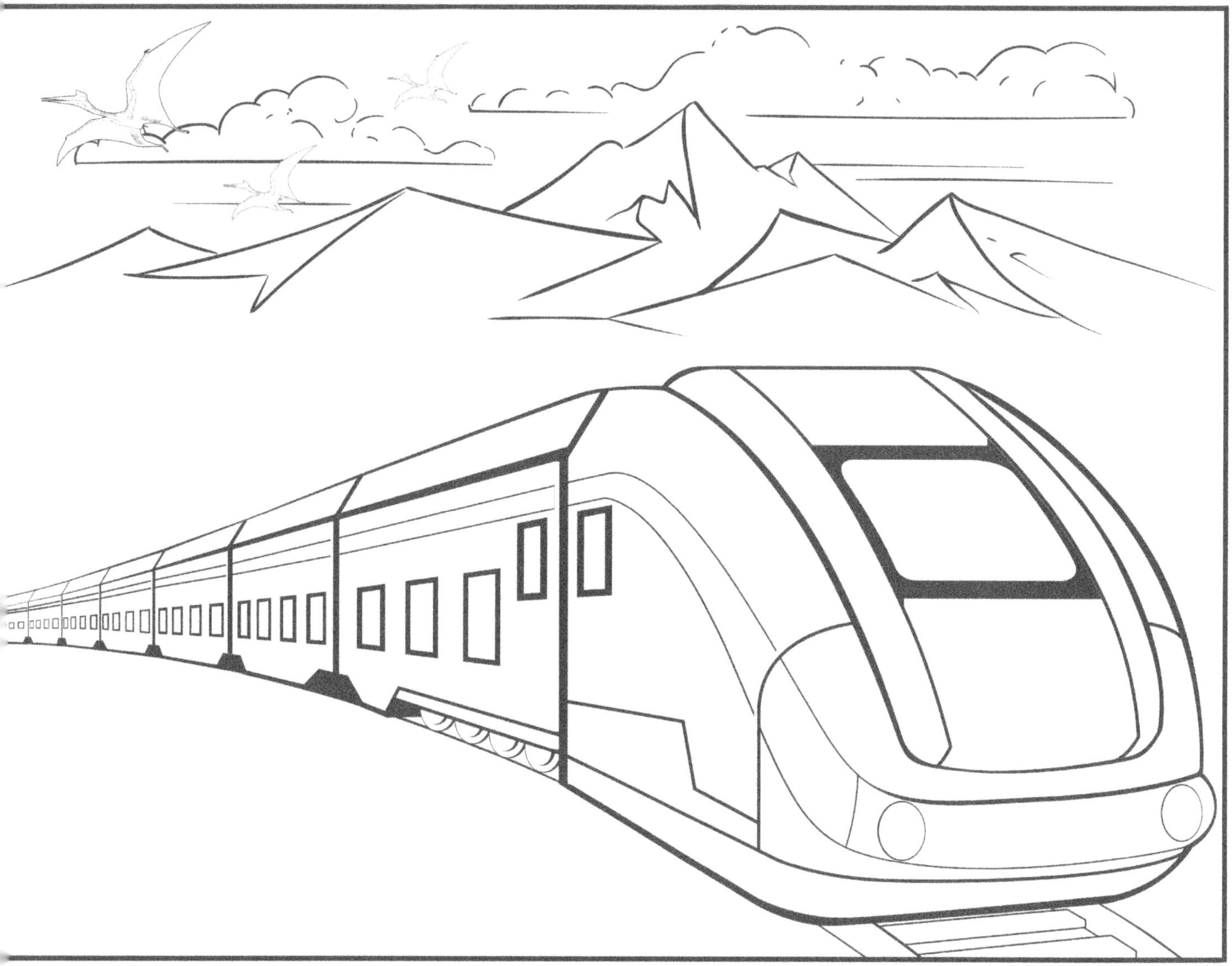

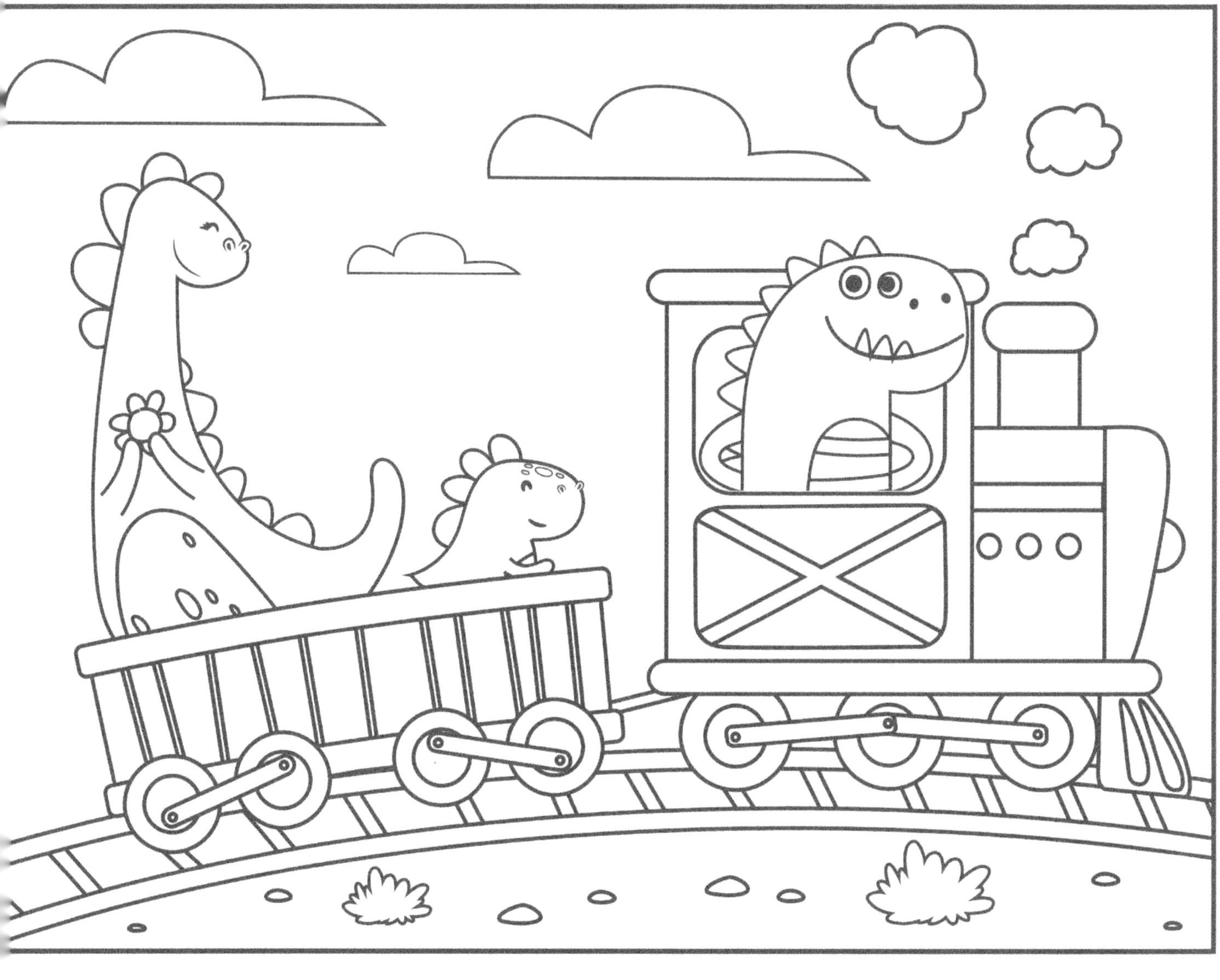

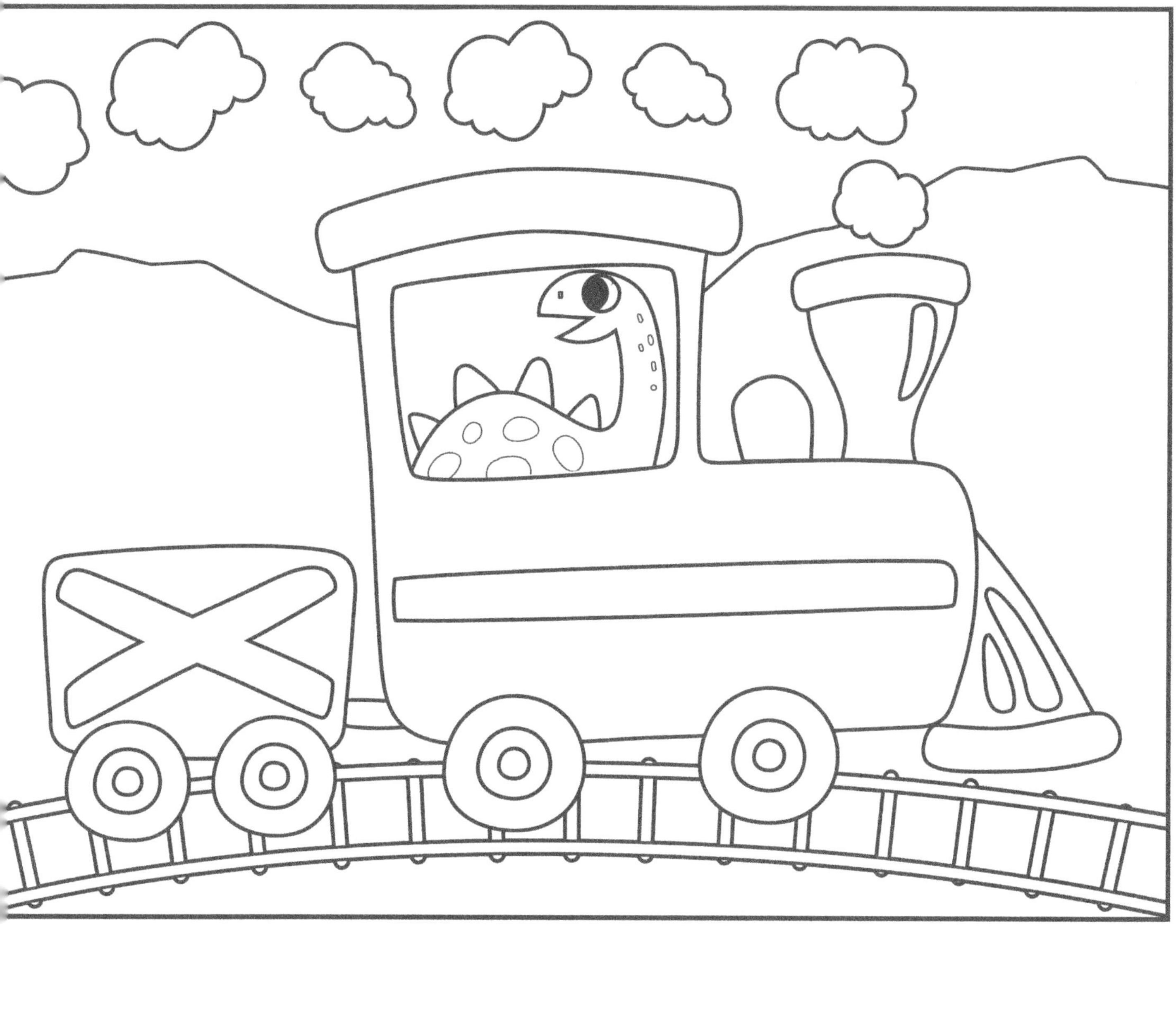

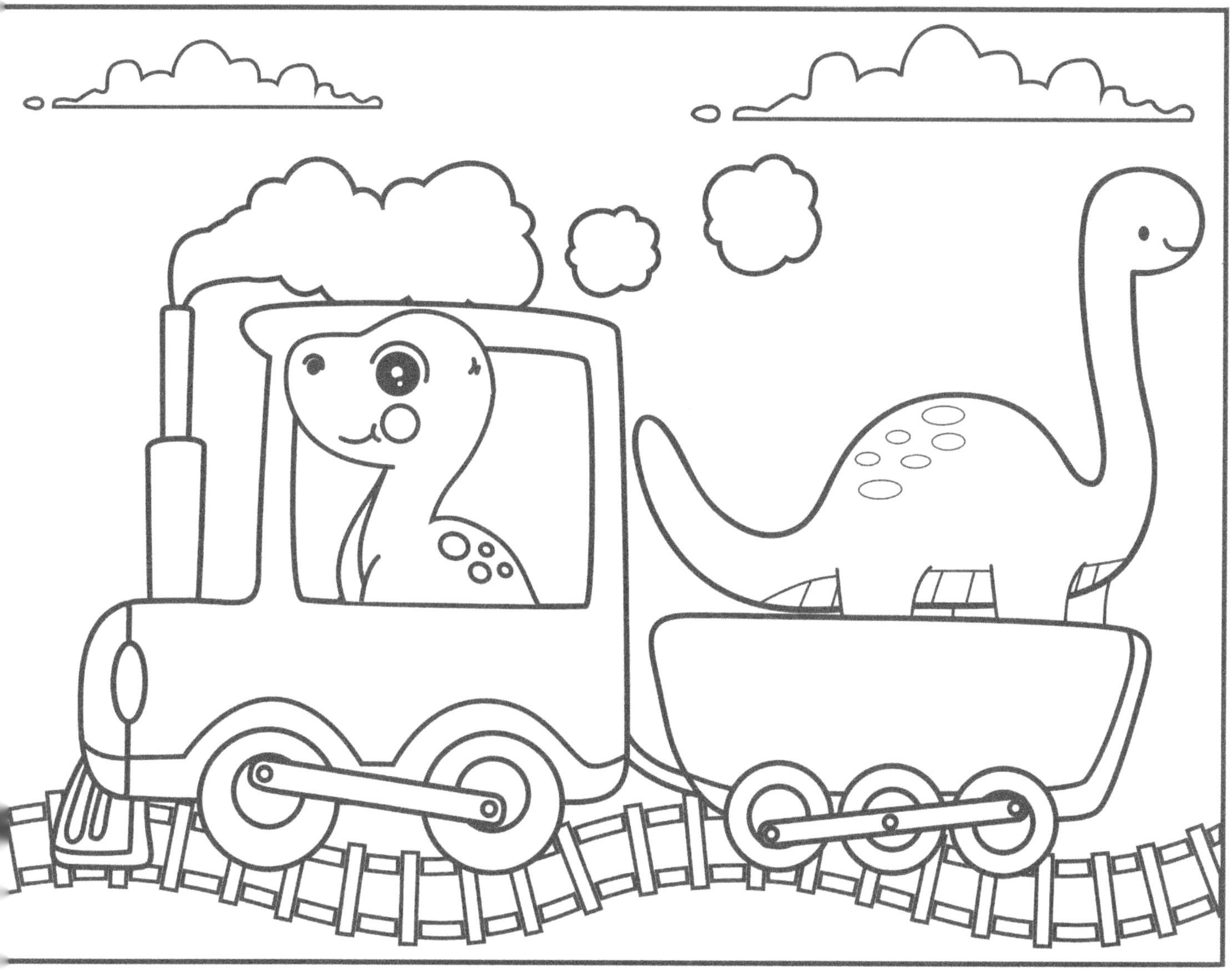

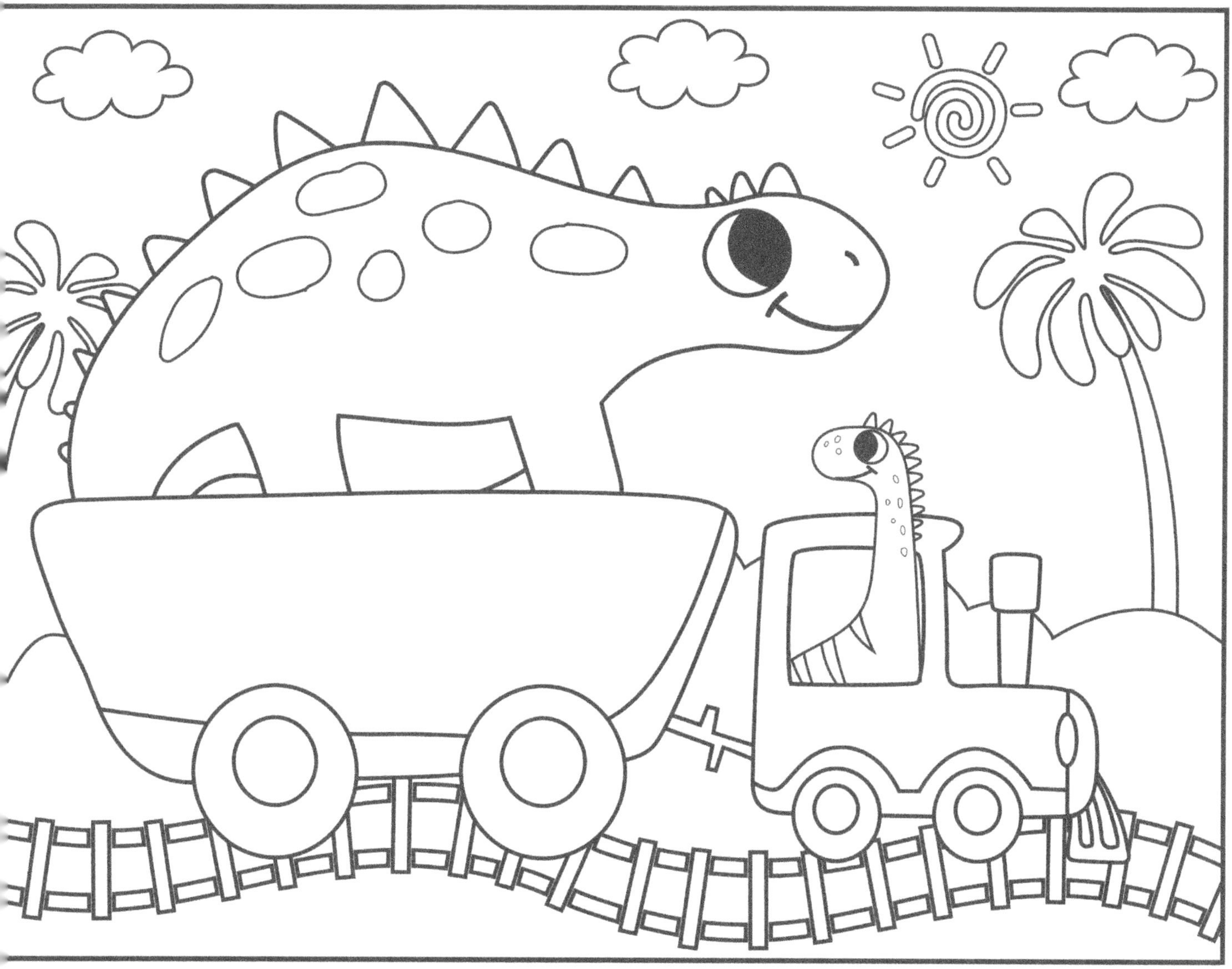

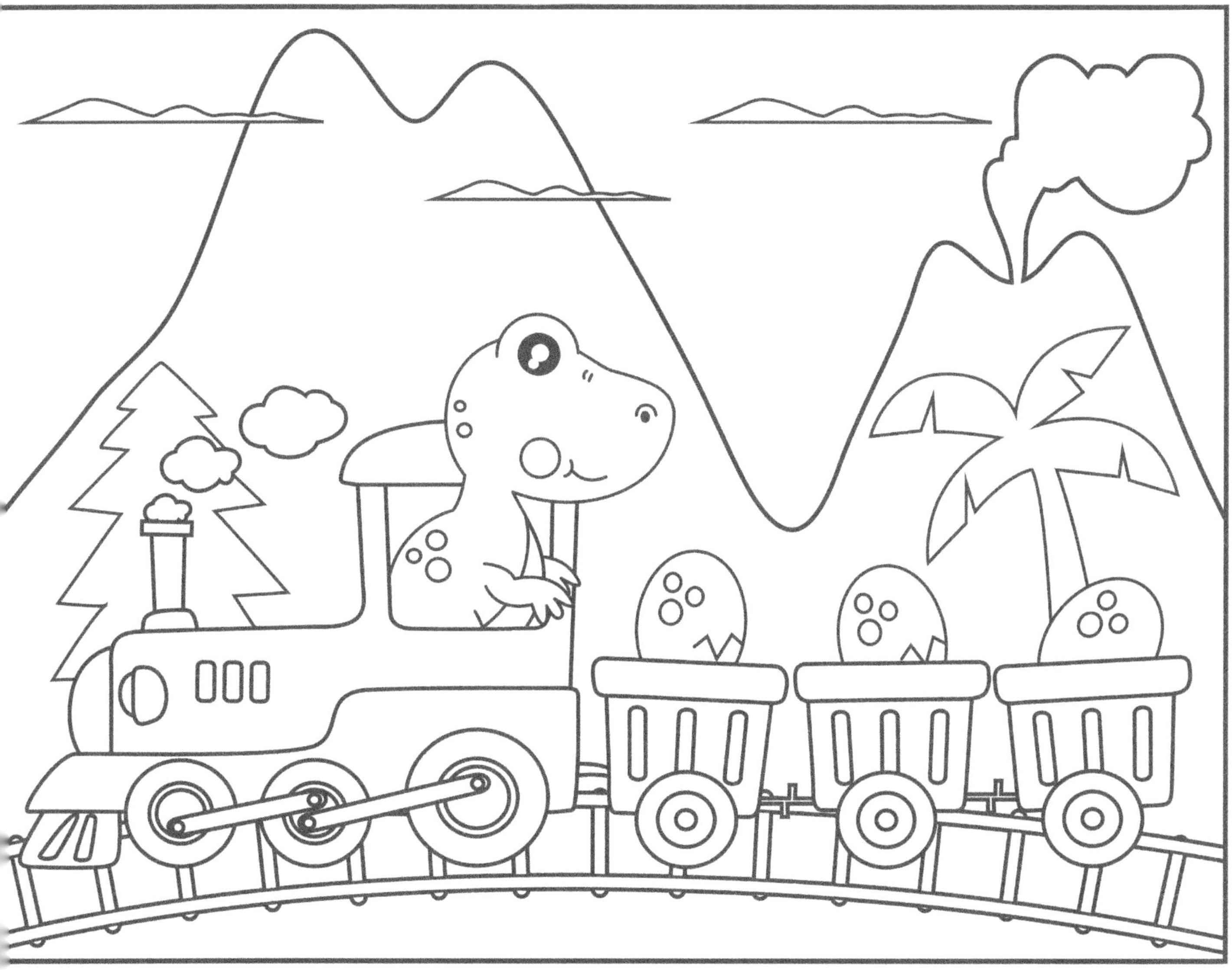

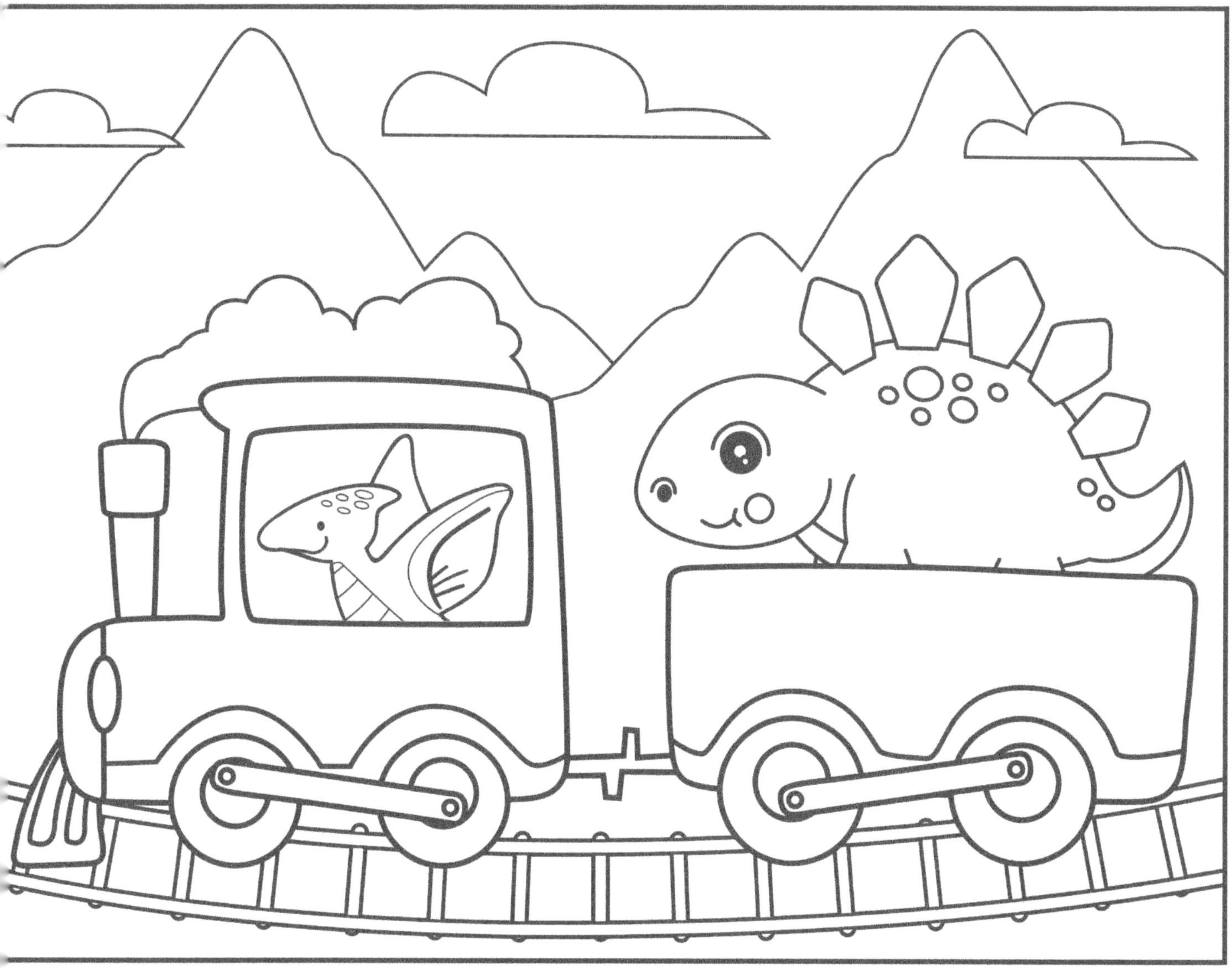

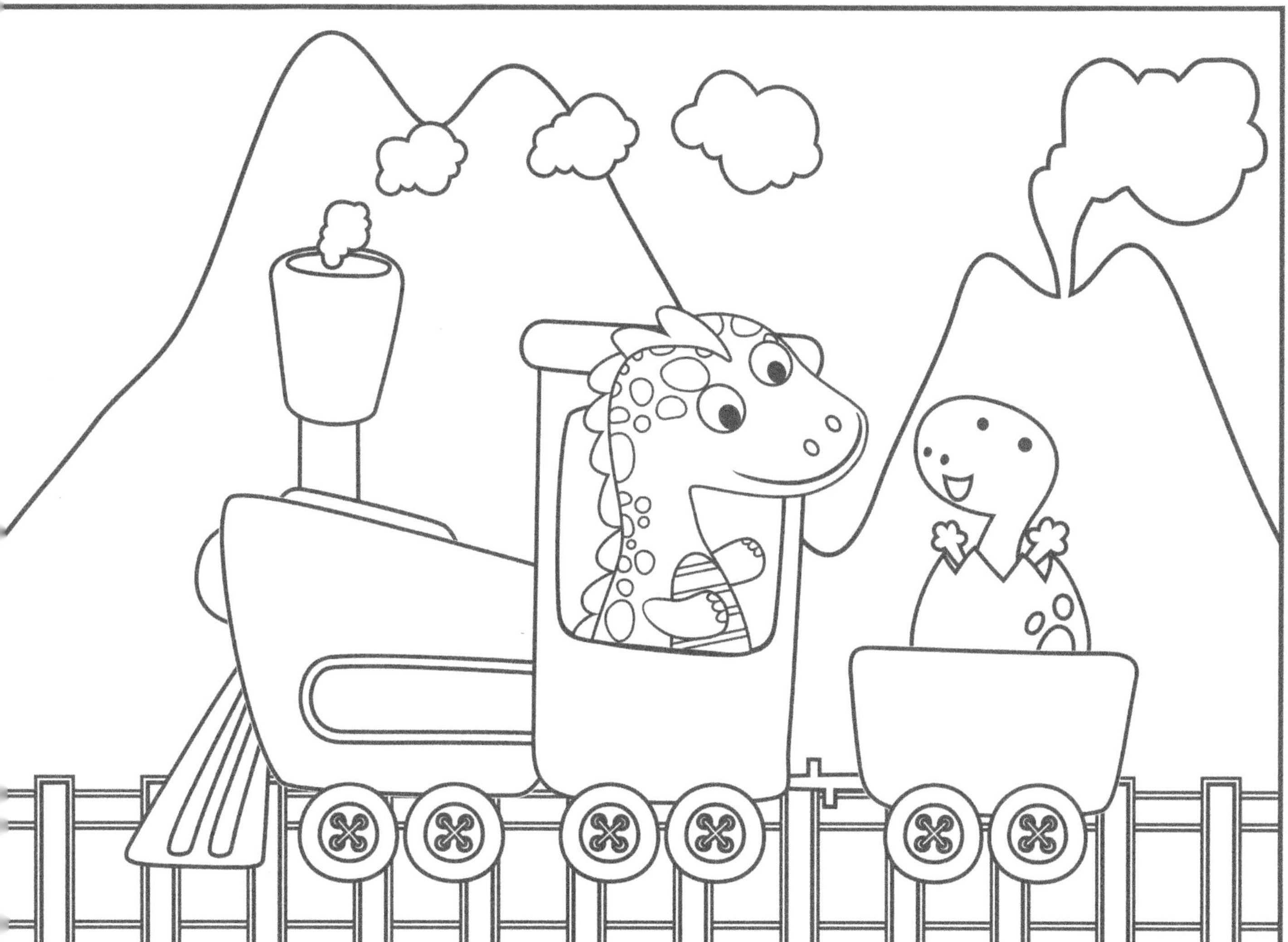

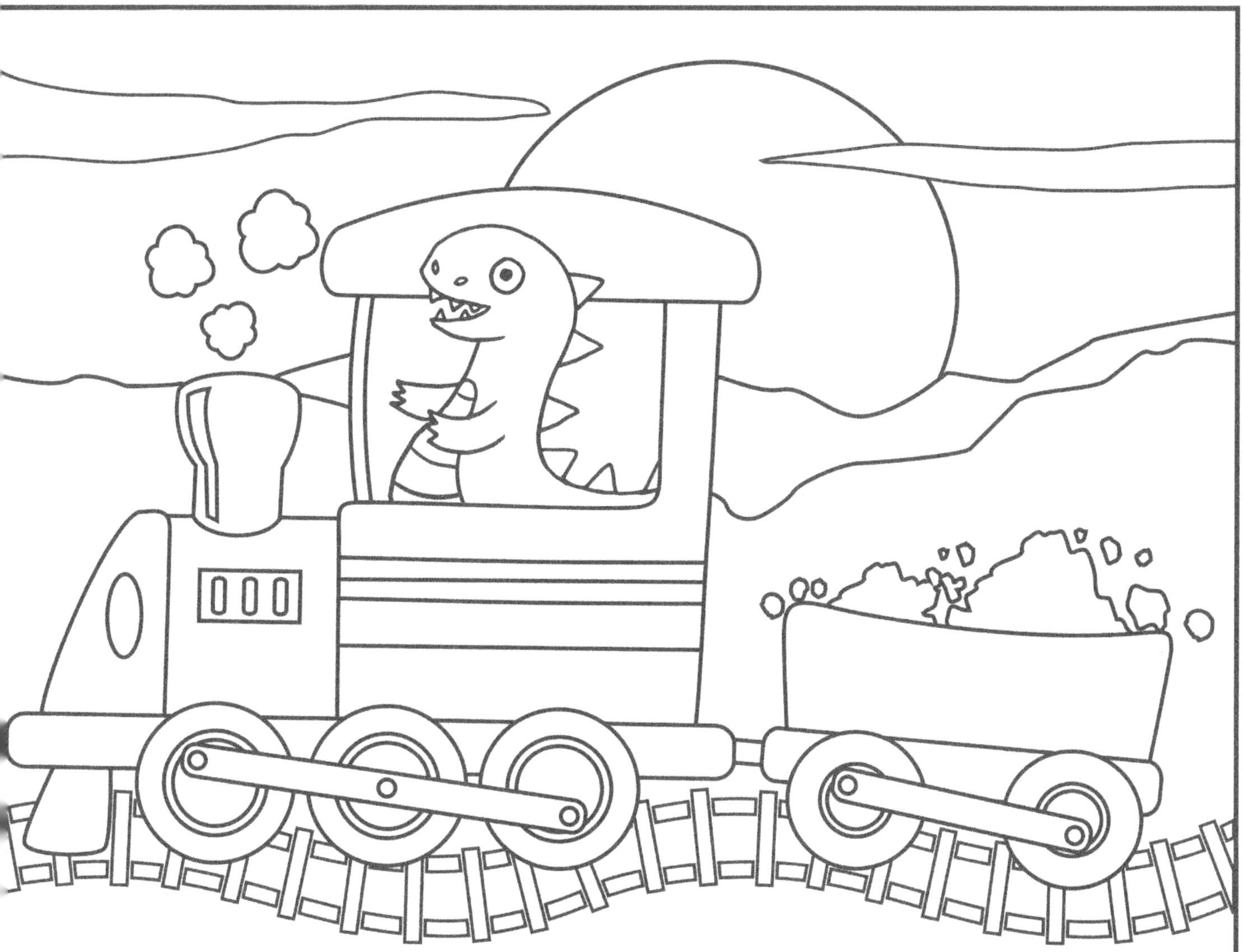

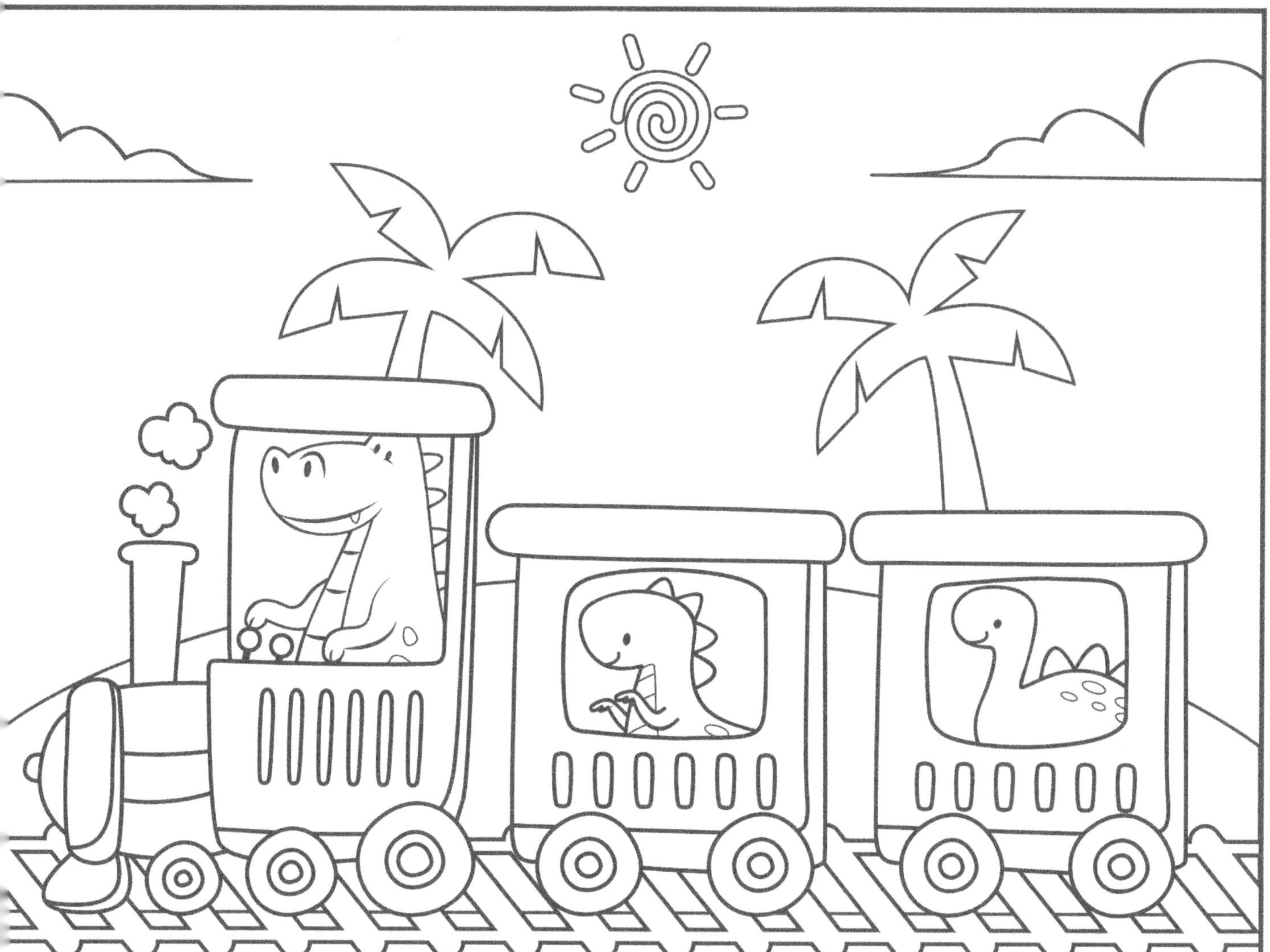

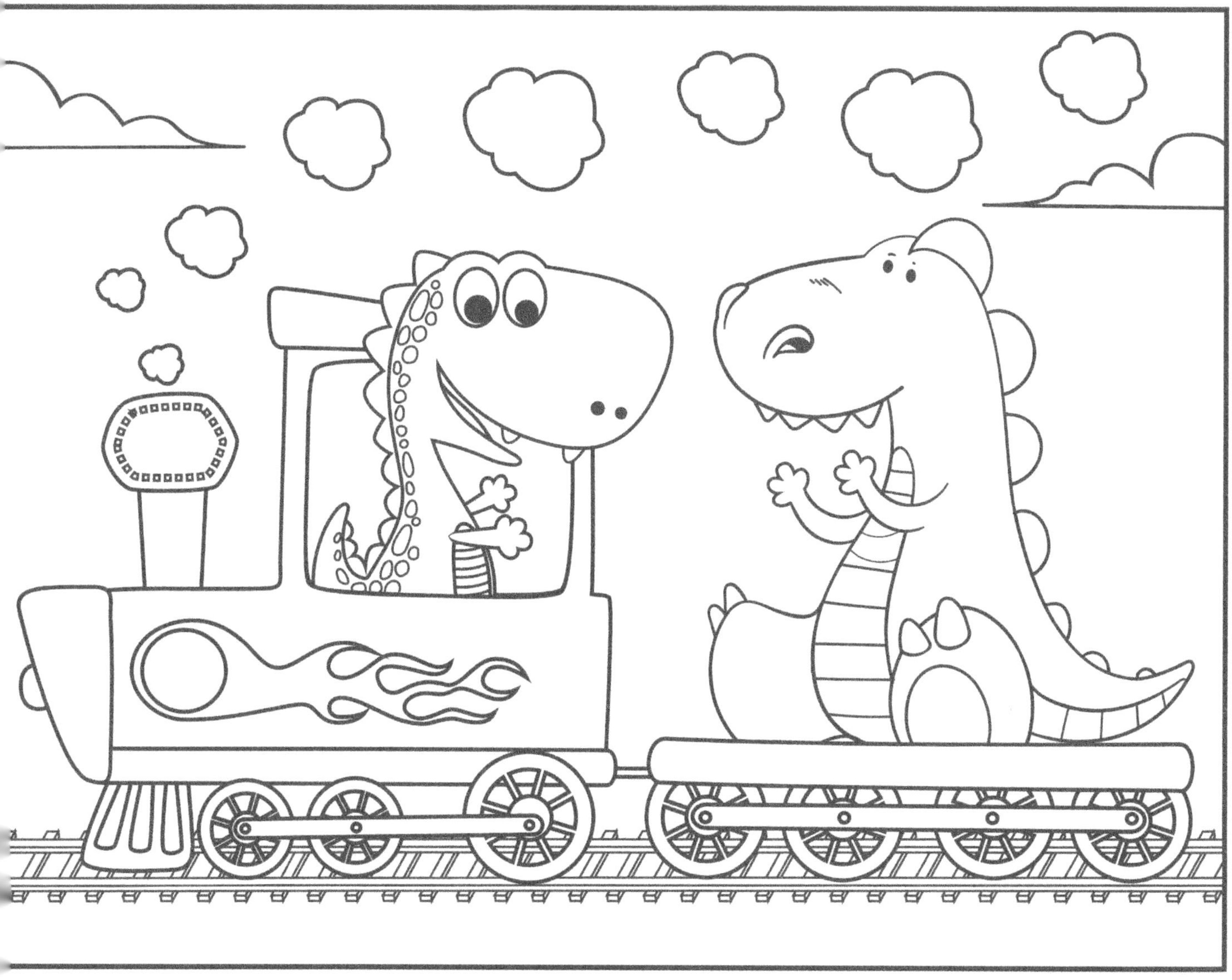

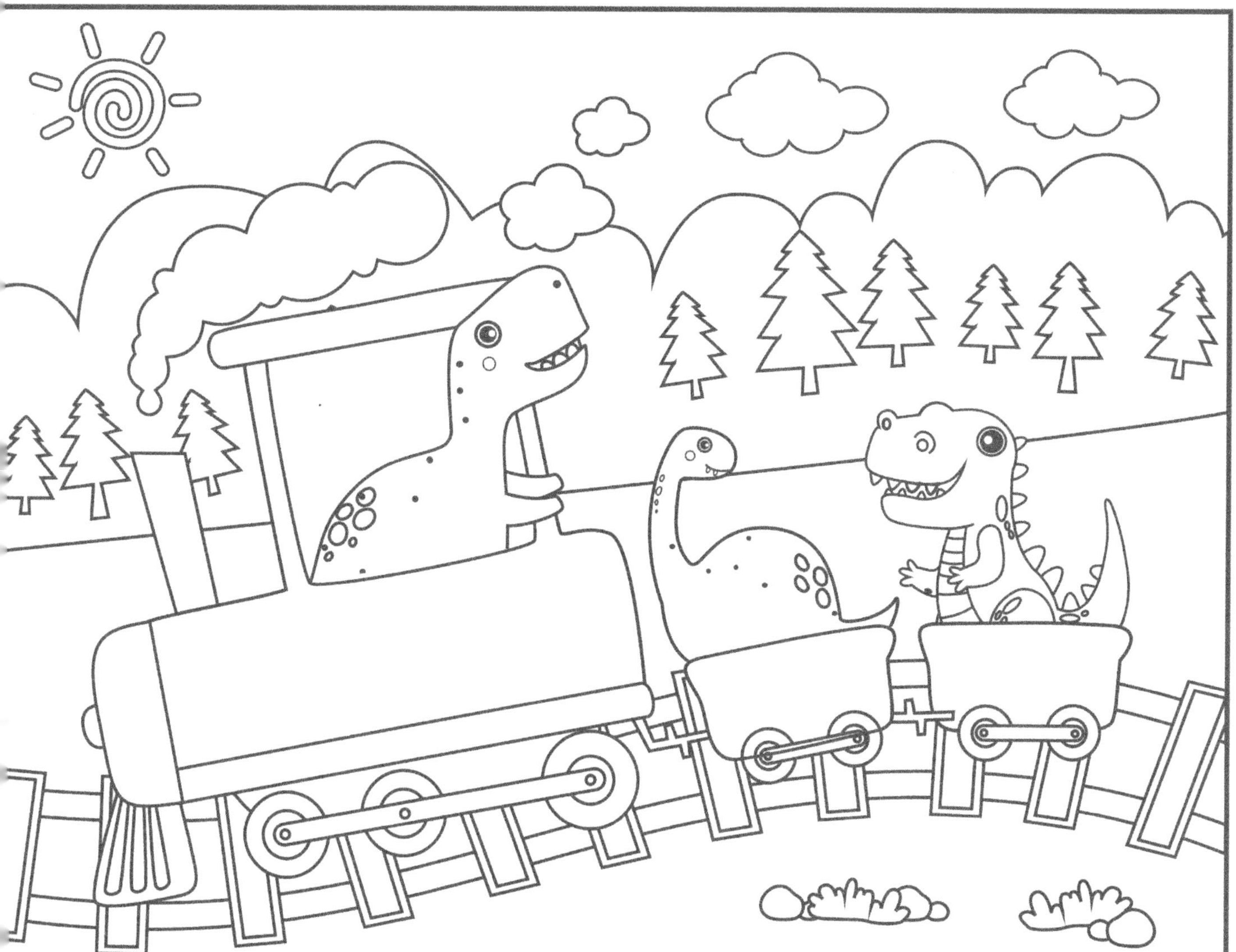

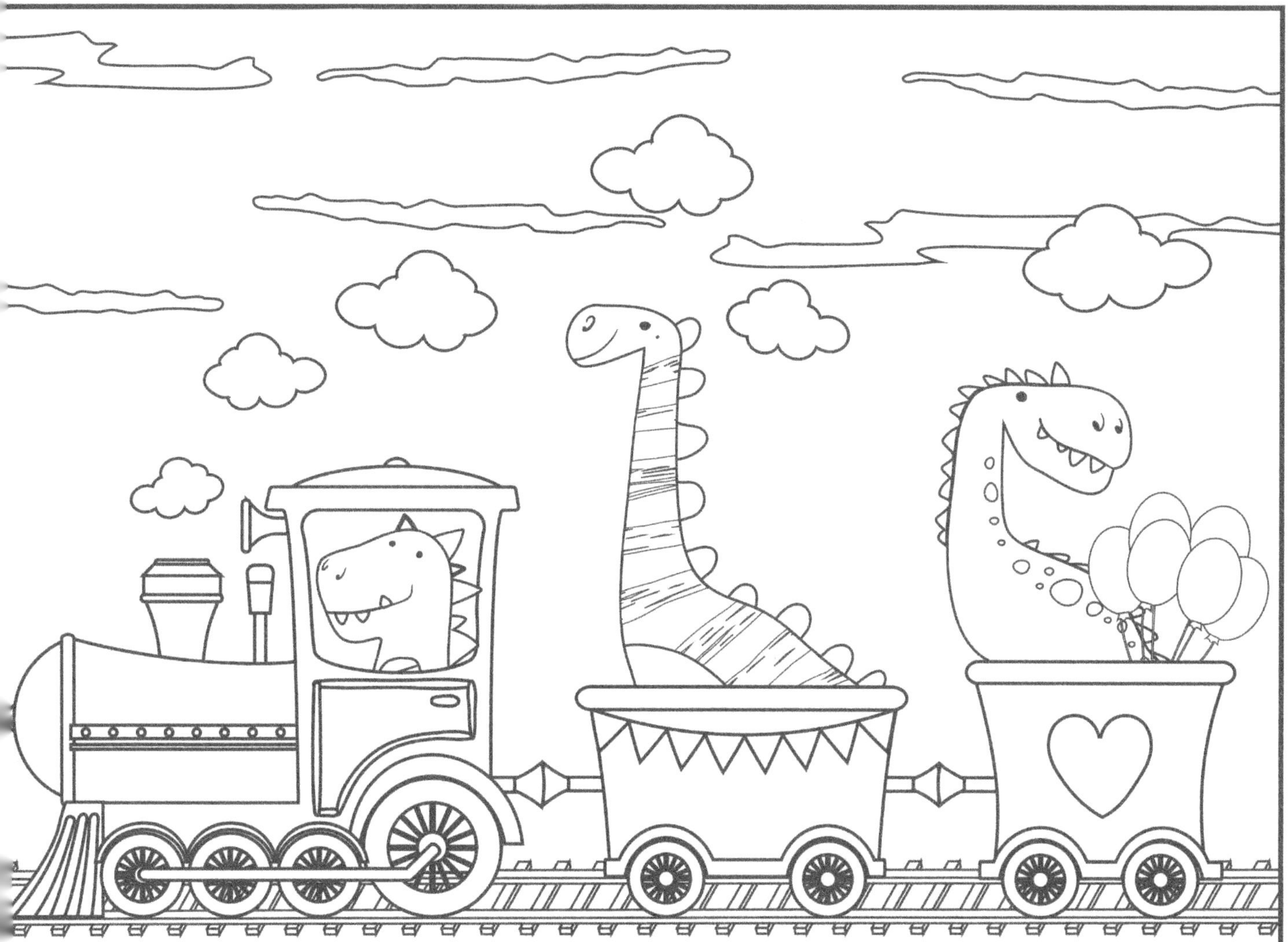

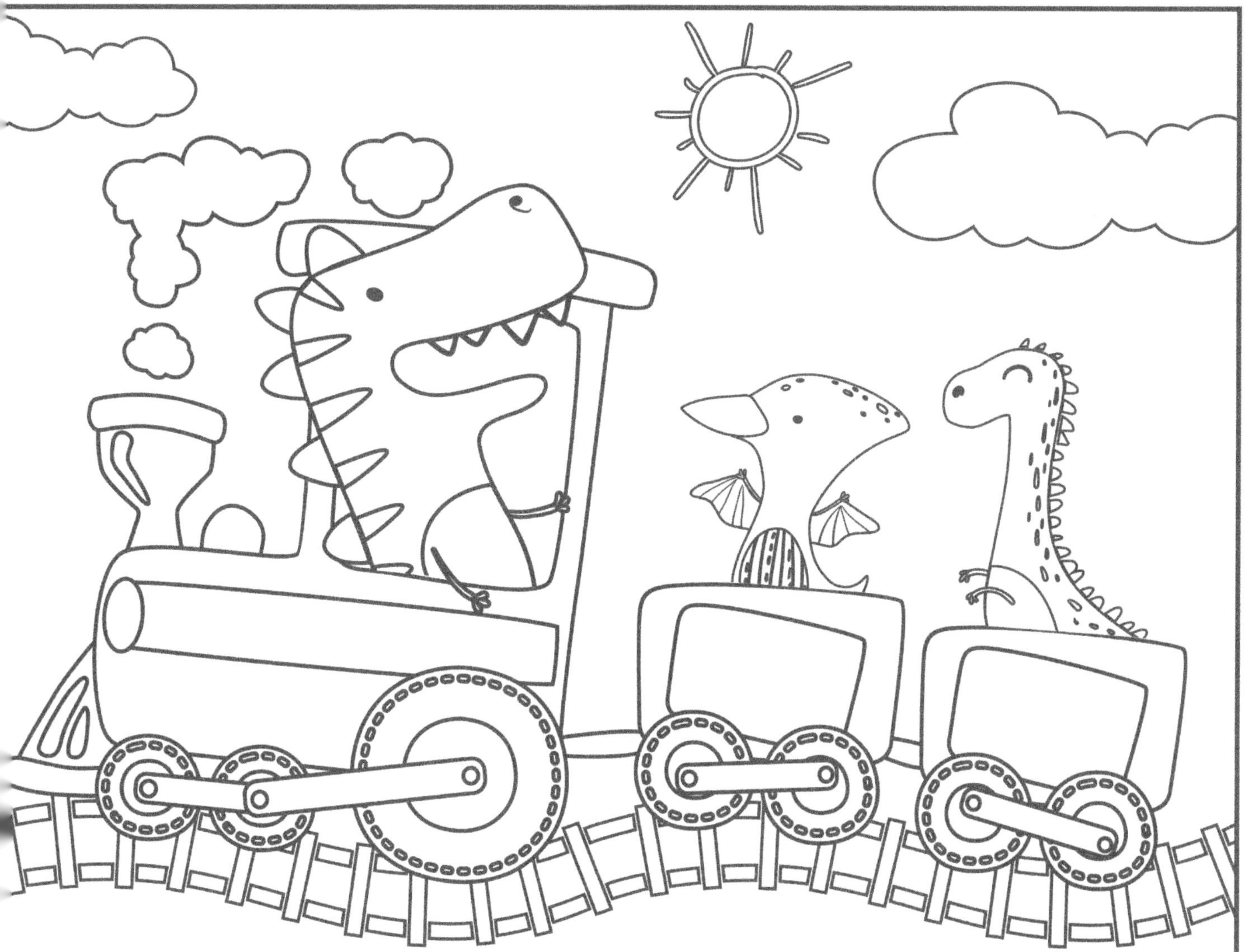

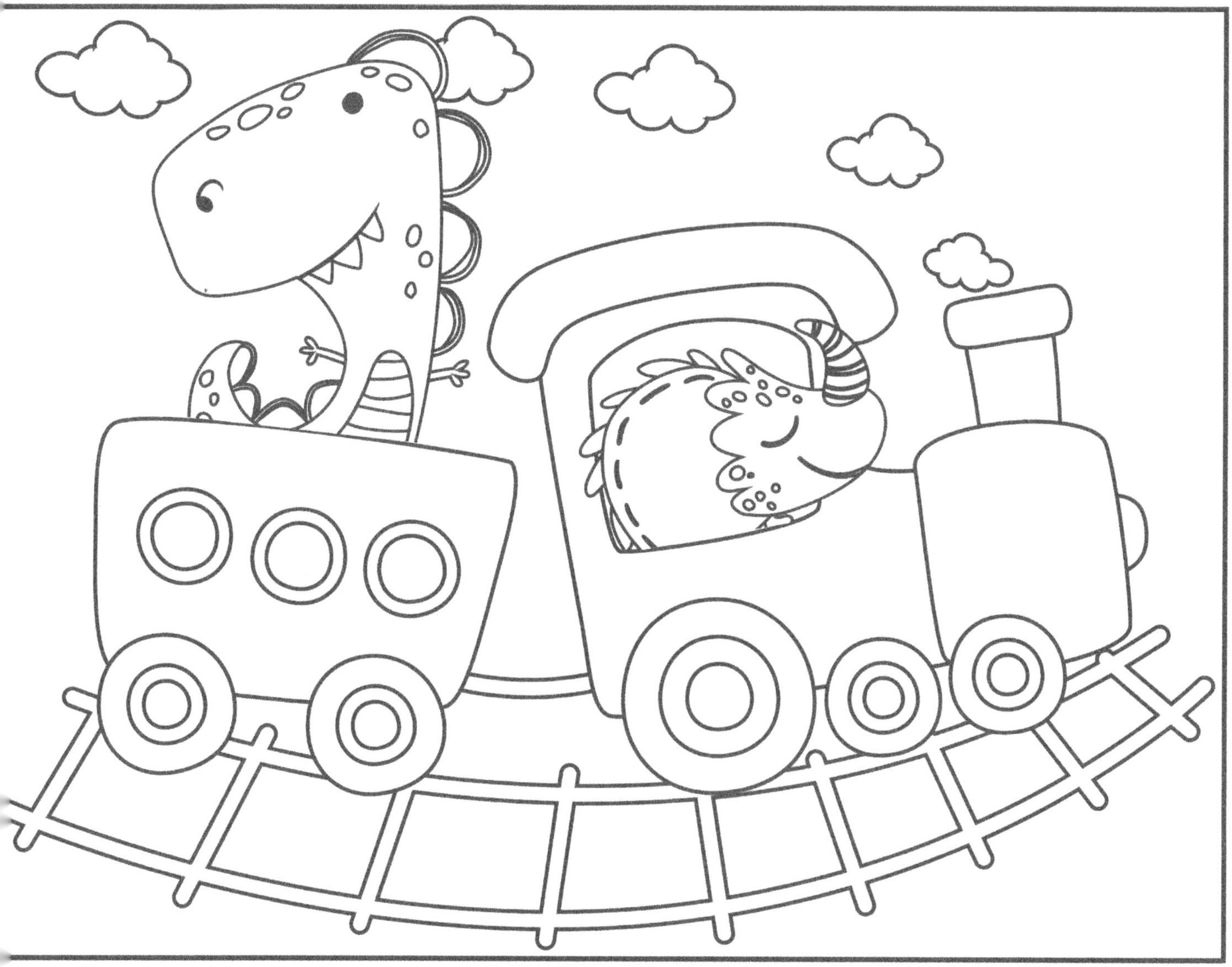

Printed in the USA
CPSIA information can be obtained
at www.ICGtesting.com
CBHW061437130824
13128CB00020B/1006

9 798211 079489